INDIAN WARRIORS and their WEAPONS

GRAY-WOLF

INDIAN
WARRIORS
and their
WEAPONS

written and illustrated by
ROBERT HOFSINDE
(Gray-Wolf)

Morrow Junior Books
New York

by the same author:

INDIAN COSTUMES
INDIAN SIGN LANGUAGE

15 16 17 18 19 20 21 22 23 24

CONTENTS

1

WARS AND WARRIORS

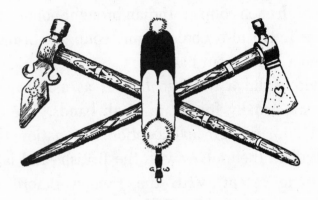

In early times there was little fighting among the American Indians. The hunters did not go far afield, and therefore they did not know that other tribes existed. As overhunting reduced the amount of game, however, the Indians began to move in search of better hunting grounds. Eventually they met other people, who perhaps claimed the same hunting rights, and fighting began. Later the Indians obtained horses, and those tribes that had few or none raided their neighbors for them. Such raids also caused wars.

In war a man might gain honor and glory. By touching an enemy in battle a warrior "counted coup." *Coup* is a French word, meaning a blow, and with each coup an Indian brought honor upon himself. He also could count coup by bringing home a horse from battle.

Rarely did a tribe go to war as a full army; Indians usually fought in small bands. The Iroquois Indians were an exception. As a nation, they had allied themselves with the British—and later, to some extent, with the French—before the American Revolution. Perhaps the largest group of Indians to fight as one great army was the combined force of Sioux and Cheyenne that met General Custer at the Little Big Horn River in 1876. Had the American Indian tribes been able to band together against the early invasions of the white man, instead of fighting among themselves, our history might have been quite different.

2
THE OJIBWA WAR TRAILS

THE Indians known today as the Ojibwa, or Chippewa, originally called themselves Anishinabe. This name means first men or original men, as did most tribal names at one time. The names that the tribes bear today were given to them by other Indians or by the early white men.

The Ojibwa lived in Minnesota, Wisconsin, and Michigan, and they were the largest tribe in that region. Others were the Fox, Sioux, and Cheyenne

Indians, and the Iroquois invaded the territory from time to time, too. Each of these tribes wanted the best hunting and fishing areas, as well as possession of the streams where wild rice grew, and they were willing to fight for these rights. They also went on the war trail to get revenge or to gain personal honor.

Scattered over vast forest areas, the Ojibwa fought their neighbors in small groups. Although they were often outnumbered by their foes, they were very fierce and successful fighters. After the Ojibwa obtained firearms from the French, around 1664, they drove the Cheyenne and the Sioux west across the Mississippi River. They drove the Fox to the south. A battle is recorded in which twenty-seven Ojibwa fought off more than one hundred Sioux.

In spring and summer the foliage of trees and bushes helped to shield the warriors as they approached their enemies, so these seasons were the usual ones for making war. An Ojibwa small war party was usually made up of volunteers, who gathered under a good leader. Whenever a large party was needed, messengers went to other Ojibwa villages and presented gifts of tobacco to the warriors there. If the warriors accepted the gifts, they set out from their own village and met the appointed war chief at a chosen location.

Unlike most Plains tribes, the Ojibwa did not wear their best costumes in battle, but reserved them for the dances that followed. On the war trail, leggings, breechclout, and moccasins were their standard apparel. Over his arm a warrior carried a soft tanned hide robe to protect himself from the cold and to sleep in at night. These robes were eventually replaced by colorful wool trade blankets. At first the Ojibwa draped the blanket over their shoulders, but later they copied the French trappers and made a loose-fitting, hooded coat out of it. The coat was held in place with a belt of the same material, and the point of the hood was usually decorated with an eagle feather or with a few streamers of brightly colored ribbon.

The Ojibwa warrior wore his hair in two long braids, but before he went off to battle he gath-

11

GRAY-WOLF.

ered part of his hair into a scalp lock. He selected a large tuft of hair on top of his head and braided about half of it. Then he wound the braid with a strip of basswood or moosewood bark to make it stand erect. After cloth came into use, bright red cloth took the place of the bark strips. The unbraided half of the tuft of hair fell loosely over the wrapping, creating the effect of a small umbrella.

A brave warrior who had counted coup by taking scalps wore an eagle feather, tipped with a strip of red flannel or a tuft of white horsehair that had been dyed red. It was usually tied to his hair in back. There were three grades of coups. For the first grade, the feather stood upright, for the second it extended horizontally, and for the third it hung loosely. One feather was worn for each scalp taken. If the warrior wore a feather split down the middle, it meant that he had been wounded in battle. After the Indians obtained guns, a feather with a large red spot painted upon it showed that the wearer had been wounded by a musket ball.

The most outstanding head ornament worn by the Ojibwa warrior was the deer-tail roach. This symbol of a great warrior was worn in battle as well as on festive occasions. Made from stiff moose hairs, porcupine hairs, and the white hairs from a deer's tail, the roach stood erect, like a mane, over the top of the warrior's head.

To make a roach the Indian gathered the strands of hair, which were about twelve inches long, into bunches about one eighth of an inch in diameter. He folded each bunch in half and tied it just above the bend, leaving a small loop at the base. Then he sewed the bunches onto the edge of a foundation, side by side in three or four rows. The foundation was made of skin, and was long, oval-shaped, and rather pointed at one end.

In the center of the foundation, the Indian placed a piece of thin bone or rawhide, which kept the roach hairs from drooping inward. He set or tied a bone socket to this spreader, and placed a feather, which twirled in the slightest breeze, in it.

The Ojibwa then made an opening near the

14

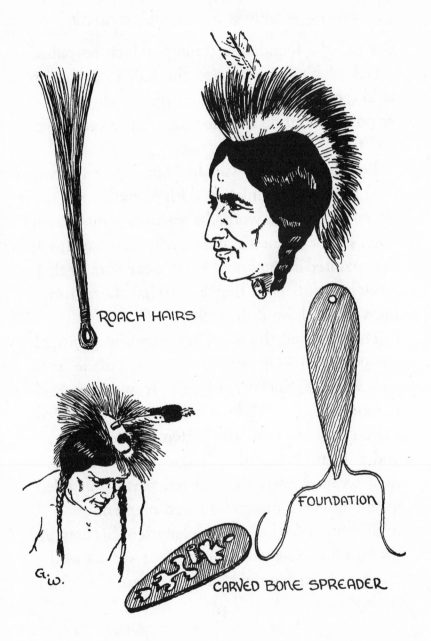

ROACH HAIRS

FOUNDATION

G.W.

CARVED BONE SPREADER

front of the foundation through which he pulled a lock of his hair. He tied the hair in a knot to hold the front of the roach in place. At the back, or pointed end he fastened long buckskin thongs and tied them around his neck.

Before he went to war the Ojibwa warrior covered his face completely with vermillion paint. When no shirt was worn, the warriors painted each other's back with a white clay. After the clay dried, they painted designs on it in various colors, or they scratched designs in the clay so that the warrior's brown skin showed through.

The bow and the war club were the principal weapons of the Ojibwa. The bow was made from well-seasoned hickory or ash. It was flat and tapered at the ends. The warrior usually decorated the back of his bow. He heated a pointed stone, and with it he traced a design in the wood. He then scraped away the charred parts, and filled in the indented design with red pigments.

Each man determined the length of his bow by his own measurements. He made it as long as the distance from his right shoulder across his chest and outstretched left arm to the tips of the fingers on his left hand. The average bow was between forty-six and forty-eight inches long, powerful enough to send a well-aimed arrow through the side of a deer.

Bowstrings were usually made from twisted sinew of moose or deer. Some bows were strung with the skin from a snapping turtle's neck. The skin was cut into a long spiral, and the strip thus produced was twisted into a cord. Such a bowstring lasted a very long time, and it would not stretch or shrink, no matter what the weather was.

Much of the Ojibwa warrior's free time was devoted to making arrows, for he always needed them. Ojibwa arrows were shorter than those made by the Plains tribes. A short arrow was better suited for use in the forest, as it was less apt to catch on branches and bushes. Also, an Ojibwa usually took aim from a kneeling position, in which it was more difficult to draw a long arrow. The arrow shafts were wood, tipped with points of bone, antler, flint, or quartz. Flint was the most common. Feathered with eagle or hawk feathers, a well-made arrow was capable of traveling 500 feet.

The arrow quiver was made of stiff buckskin, and it had a broad carrying strap. The strap rested over the warrior's right shoulder, passing across his chest and under his left arm. When in position, the quiver hung against his left shoulder blade in an upright position, so that the warrior could draw arrows over his shoulder with his right hand.

The Ojibwa also used war clubs of various types. Perhaps the most unusual and original was the one made by nature, with only a little help from the Indian. To make it, a man selected a young, pliable sapling growing near his home, which he tied into a knot close to the ground. After a season of growth, the soft, young bark broke its fibers where it had been knotted, and a solid knob formed there. The sapling continued to grow out of the knob, and after it reached the desired size, the Indian cut it off close to the ground. He then cut the trunk to the proper length for a handle.

To make another type of club, the Indian dug a young tree, roots and all, out of the soil. From the root ball he trimmed the longest root shoots, and he cut off the top of the tree leaving enough trunk to form the handle. Finally he hung the club above the hot coals in his lodge so it would dry hard and firm. Once it was dry, the man trimmed the protruding side roots to a uniform length and whittled them to sharp points.

After the French established trading posts, the

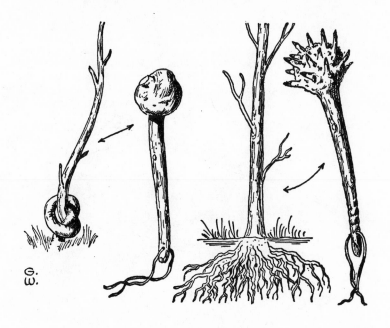

Indians obtained knives, tomahawks, saw blades, files, and other useful items. With these tools they were able to make new types of war clubs, and one model was particularly popular among the Ojibwa. Shaped much like a gunstock, the narrow end of the club formed the grip, or handle. The upper, broader section held either a sharp stone point or from one to three sharp points made by inserting the blades from butcher knives.

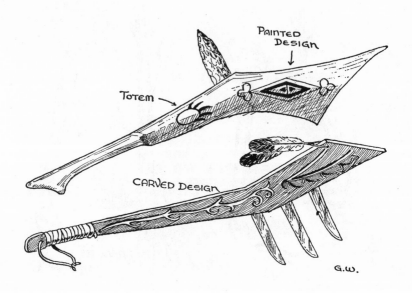

PAINTED DESIGN

TOTEM

CARVED DESIGN

G.W.

The Ojibwa early allied themselves with the French. First they supplied them with furs, and later they fought with them against the English. An Ojibwa could get a good flintlock gun at a French trading post for two beaver pelts. The English, however, were not as generous with their allies, the Iroquois and the Sioux.

Personal bravery was not lacking among the Ojibwa. In one case, which is recorded, a small group of hunters were attacked by a large number of Sioux. Telling his companions to flee, one of the Ojibwa took a stand behind a fallen tree, and there he held back the Sioux as he sent arrow after arrow in their direction.

His first shot killed one of the Sioux, which checked the onrush for a moment. The Sioux continued to shoot at the lone Ojibwa, but their aim was short. Another arrow from the Ojibwa's bow wounded a Sioux, and in the confusion that followed the Ojibwa quickly gathered up the Sioux arrows close to him and sprinted away after his friends.

In a moment the Sioux were after him. When

he came to another place where he could shield himself, he took his stand once more and began to shoot at the Sioux with their own arrows. Several times he gathered up the arrows around him, fled to a new position, and held the enemy off. His friends managed to escape, but at last one of the Sioux warriors' arrows found its mark, killing the Ojibwa. When the escaping Ojibwa returned to their own village they raised a war party, as was customary, and they avenged the death of the lone Ojibwa soon after.

During the spring and summer the Ojibwa held their dances as well as making war. In them the men described their past war deeds in action and in oratory, giving fresh courage to warriors and stirring young men to follow the examples of their elders.

At these dances the Ojibwa appeared in their finest costumes. In early days they painted designs on their garments. Later they embroidered them with moose hair, and finally they decorated them with the imported trade beads. By early 1800 costumes were made of black and dark-blue

velvet and broadcloth. On the dark background flower-and-leaf bead designs, made with beads of light and dark green, light blue, shades of red and pink, white, lavender, and yellow, looked striking and colorful.

Velvet leggings bore beaded floral designs. They began at the bottom of the leg and, like a growing vine, wound upward the full length of the legging. Breechclouts, also of velvet, were decorated to match the leggings. A shirt jacket with a velvet yoke and cuffs was often made from broadcloth. It, too, was decorated with beads. Years later the shirt was replaced by a vest cut on the style of the white man's, but beaded front and back.

Warriors of high rank wore the roach; other warriors had otter-skin turbans. Often a single feather stood upright at one side near the back. The Ojibwa moccasin had a beaded velvet top and, perhaps, a beaded cuff.

The warriors wore bead necklaces, garters, and a sash, and they carried a large pouch, called a bandolier, over their shoulders. These bags were

also made of velvet, frequently backed with broadcloth. The upper third of the bandolier had a beaded floral design through which the velvet background showed, and the lower two thirds consisted of a large, square piece of beadwork on a white-bead background.

The Ojibwa took great pride in his appearance at all the ceremonial functions. Even the large, hanging dance drum had a skirt of beautiful beadwork.

WAR DRUM WITH SKIRT

3

THE IROQUOIS WARRIOR

THE confederacy of the Iroquois, called the Five
Nations, was formed, in part, to keep peace among
the member tribes. It consisted of the Mohawk,
Cayuga, Onondaga, Oneida, and Seneca tribes.
Around 1722 the Tuscarora from the Carolinas
joined the Longhouse, after having been driven
out of their own land by the white men. As the
Tuscarora were of Iroquois linguistic stock, they
were readily admitted by the original members,

and the name of the league was changed to the Six Nations. Other tribes belonging to the Iroquois were not included in the confederacy and were, in fact, often at war with its members. The Huron to the north and the Cherokee of the Carolinas were two such groups.

The Iroquois lived in northern New York. As warriors, they were so fierce that by the end of the seventeenth century they controlled the land, and many of the tribes, from the Ottawa River in Ohio south to the Cumberland River in Tennessee, and westward from Maine to Lake Michigan. They made friends with the early Dutch, from whom they obtained firearms, and with these new weapons of war they became even bolder. Iroquois moccasins left imprints as far west as the Black Hills of South Dakota. The warriors fought the Catawbas in South Carolina, and they invaded the villages of the Creeks in Florida.

Small war parties set forth to gain personal glory, and at times a single warrior took to the trail for the same reason. On such raiding trips, often many days' journey from camp, any man who wished to was free to leave the party and return home. This decision did not in any way disgrace him in the eyes of the others, although among other tribes such an act would have branded the man as a coward.

Most Indians usually formed small war parties under a leader, but the Iroquois often mustered large armies. In 1654, for example, a party of 1800 Iroquois attacked a village of the Erie, a Pennsylvania tribe of Iroquois blood, which had between 3000 and 4000 warriors. So fiercely did the New York Iroquois fight that even against such odds they were victorious. At another time in their bloody history, a party of Mohawk and Seneca Indians numbering close to 1000 invaded the Huron north of Toronto, Canada. In two days of fighting they burned two Huron towns, took untold captives, and returned home with much loot.

Captives, including men, women, and children, were always taken on such raids. The captive men replaced Iroquois husbands or sons lost in battle. The children were adopted into families, and the captive women often married into the tribe. Those not so fortunate became slaves, working the fields for the women and doing much of the other hard labor. Captives served to keep the tribe large and strong, and as most of them were of Iroquois stock they adapted quite readily to their new life.

The winters in northern New York are often harsh and cold, with long-lasting snows. For that reason the Iroquois dressed far more warmly than did the Indians to the south of them. They wore a buckskin shirt reaching down over their thighs, leggings, breechclout, and moccasins. In very cold weather they draped an animal robe, tanned with the fur left on, over their head and shoulders.

During warmer weather, when the buckskin shirt was discarded, the Iroquois wore a short, wraparound kilt to cover the exposed upper thighs where the front and back of the breechclout did not come together. A belt of deerskin, wound around the waist twice and tied in front, held the warrior's club and his scalping knife.

Old men and medicine men had long hair, but

GRAY·WOLF.

the warriors shaved, plucked, or singed theirs off, leaving only a short, manelike crest of hair on top of their head. On the actual war trail the Iroquois warrior often wore a deertail roach like that of his everlasting enemy, the Ojibwa.

Before the Indians had firearms the Iroquois wore a breast armor to ward off arrows. It was made from woven willow branches and protected the warrior from neck to thighs. Shields were also made from woven willows, and then covered with thick buckskin. Both the shield and breast armor were discarded after guns came into use, for they proved useless against musket balls.

The principal weapon of the Iroquois warrior in long-range fighting was a short bow. He tipped his arrows with flint or quartz points, and carried them in quivers made from braided corn husk, elm bark, or buckskin. He also used spears, which were tipped with long, slender stone points.

For close fighting the Iroquois had war clubs, which were beautifully made. The simplest kind consisted of a long handle ending in a ball. Often the ball was skillfully carved to represent a human head. Some warriors made even more elaborate clubs and added the head of a wolf or a bear, with its open jaw clamping down on the large carved ball. Other clubs ended in an oversized bird, worked in the finest detail, holding the ball in its claws or talons.

The Iroquois used stone-headed war clubs, too, as did many other tribes, and a club shaped like a gunstock, similar to that of the Ojibwa. The iron

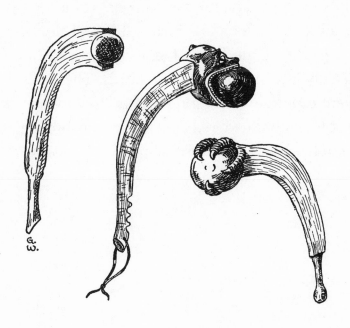

tomahawk from the trading post was a welcome weapon to the Iroquois. Once they had obtained it, they soon learned to throw it with great accuracy and dexterity at any moving or standing target.

The early Iroquois costumes worn for war ceremonies were ornamented with quill and moosehair embroidery. When the white man made trade beads available, the old designs were copied in beadwork. Floral designs were worked on shirt cuffs, bags, and on the toes and cuffs of moccasins. Beadwork done on leggings and breechclouts was worked in single lines of graceful curved motifs, usually in white or pale-blue beads. These designs were especially widespread after 1537, when the Iroquois obtained red and dark-blue broadcloth from the English and French.

4

THE FIGHTING SIOUX

A GROUP of Sioux warriors were sitting around a small fire, smoking and talking, when their chief entered the circle. He stood for a moment looking about him, and then finally pointed silently to one of the men. That man knew the surrounding country as well as anyone could. Without a word, he got to his feet and went to his lodge. From there he emerged a short while later, ready to start on a scouting trip.

Passing by the still seated warriors, the scout now wore only a breechclout and a pair of undecorated moccasins. In his belt were his hunting knife and two pairs of extra moccasins. Around his neck, suspended from a buckskin thong, he wore a small beaded pouch containing his personal good-luck sign. His quiver full of arrows and a short, powerful bow were slung across his back, and over his left arm he carried a soft robe made from tanned deerskin. Silently he passed among the lodges, and in a few moments left the village behind.

As he walked the scout stayed well hidden, avoiding any high ground. Although he was well within his tribe's own hunting grounds, an enemy scout might be there, too. All day he traveled at a steady pace. From time to time he crawled to the rim of a high place to have a look at the country, dropping below again before continuing on his way. Nightfall found the scout near a small river, and after drinking his fill he found a good hiding place among some boulders well overgrown with brush. There he rested and slept

through the night, but at the first sign of daylight he was on the move again.

During one of his periodic climbs to a high point the Sioux saw a herd of buffalo. Watching them for a while, he began to notice that they were acting nervous and restless—not at all as a grazing herd normally acts. As he watched, the herd suddenly began to mill around, and in a short while he saw mounted men circling the shaggy beasts, bringing some of them down. He felt sure that the riders were Pawnee, great enemies of the Sioux, who had dared to enter the Sioux hunting grounds.

The scout at once retreated from his observation post and turned toward his own village. Sure that there was no one around him now, he made good time and reached the village by midafternoon. There he reported to the chief, who in turn sent a camp crier through the village to prepare the warriors for battle.

From the lodges came the men, young and middleaged, while boys brought up riding and war horses for the warriors. Many of the men wore war bonnets, while others wore their coup feathers. All were painted for war.

One man among them stood out, for he wore no head ornament of any kind, and he further called attention to himself by joining the group late. This man was regarded by the others as a coward. Whenever a war dance was held before the tribe went on the war trail, he danced well. He showed in pantomime just what he planned to do to the enemy when they met in the field. However, once the battle started this man was usually found where the fighting was the lightest. His behavior had caused much village gossip, and the time would soon arrive for challenging him.

Mounting their good riding horses and leading their trained war ponies, the Sioux followed the scout. A little after sundown they were near the lodges set up by the buffalo-hunting Pawnee. The following morning the Sioux attacked and surprised the Pawnee so much that the battle was very short. As usual, the coward held back.

On their return to the Sioux encampment the men rode around the village. They had lost only one warrior, and only one other was slightly wounded, so there was great jubilation. The widow of the slain man and his relatives, however, kept to their lodges, keening over their loss.

In the evening a victory dance was held. The victory dance was also called a scalp dance, because during it the warriors displayed the scalps they had taken. Afterward the scalps were usually burned. All the warriors who had been on the raid were at the dance, dressed exactly as they had been on the war trail. Those men who had earned coups in the battle had prepared their coup feathers before the dance. Two of the warriors wore an eagle feather standing upright behind their head. To the tip of the feather they had glued a tuft of horsehair, dyed brilliant red. Those coup feathers were of the highest order and showed that the wearers had, without any weapons in their hands, ridden in among the enemy. Doing so they had shown great bravery as well as contempt for the enemy, as they had dared to ride close enough to strike warriors with their bare hands. Other men wore a new feather that projected horizontally. It meant that they had counted coup by striking or touching a wounded enemy. One warrior had a notch cut into the edge of his feather, and by this sign everyone knew that he had cut an enemy throat. The one wounded man wore a feather dyed red to show what had befallen him.

When he had won thirty coup feathers, a Sioux had earned the right to wear a full war bonnet. If a man showed unusual courage and daring, how-

ever, his war companions could present him with a bonnet regardless of how many or how few coup feathers he had earned.

On this evening of the victory dance the coward, too, wore a feather. It had three red bars painted across it. After all, had he not struck three dead enemies?

War bonnets fluttered in the evening wind. Soft buckskin shirts and leggings showed velvety in the firelight. Quills and beads sparkled as the Sioux warriors danced. Suddenly three older women stepped out of the dark outer circle. Each had been widowed when her husband had been killed in battle. Each had been left crying when her son had followed his father to the land beyond. As they moved into the circle of firelight all could see that the middle woman carried a full war bonnet before her. Lifting it high above her head she walked around the fire, followed by her two companions. Four times they walked the circle. Then they turned their steps directly toward the great boaster, the toucher of dead enemies, and to him they presented the bonnet.

A complete hush fell over the spectators at this challenge.

Would the coward run out of the circle? If he did, he would be banned forever from the tribe and become an outcast. If he accepted the bonnet, he would have to go on the war trail at once, not returning until he could bring back proof that he was a man and a warrior.

All eyes were upon the dramatic scene. For a long moment the coward stood still, the insult sinking in deeper and deeper. Then, very slowly, he reached for the bonnet, took it, and with bowed head left the circle.

There was one other way in which a bonnet could be given as a challenge. From time to time, for various reasons, two families within the tribe feuded. Each family always tried to get the better of the other, especially in public. These feuds could last a long time before they came to a climax. On a night when the tribe had gathered for a dance, a member of one of the feuding families might step forward and present a bonnet to the young son of the other lodge.

The challenge was a brutal one, for it offered no escape. The youth had to join the next war party that was formed.

If the young man heard about the plot in advance, he could sneak out of camp before the dance. Then his enemies tried to hunt him down and bring him back.

Once the youth had accepted the bonnet, the women of his family started to keen for him. They cut off their hair or cut off a joint of a finger as a sign of mourning, for surely one so inexperienced in war could not be expected to return.

In the village as well as on a scouting trip, a Sioux man usually wore only a breechclout, though on cool days he might add a pair of leggings. His soft-tanned buffalo robe was always at his hand so that he could wrap it around himself should visitors call, or if he was summoned to a council meeting.

His war bonnet was looked upon as sacred medicine, and so was his war shirt. This shirt, trimmed with human hair or with white ermine skins, was worn only on the war trail, at dances, or in council, and then only by braves who had proved themselves in battle. Each lock of hair on the shirt represented a coup won by taking an enemy horse or a prisoner, by being wounded, or by other deeds. These shirts were erroneously called scalp shirts by early white men, for the hair used was not taken from scalps. In most cases it came from the owner's own braids or from the hair of his wife or other female relatives.

The Sioux carried a rawhide shield into battle. It could ward off an arrow, but the designs and symbols painted on its face were considered even more protective. It was another kind of medicine. Nevertheless, a shield bearer was more apt to be shot at in battle as warriors always wanted to capture an enemy shield, which was an important coup.

War societies, which were somewhat like men's clubs, existed among the various tribes. The members were warriors of proven merit, and they were usually grouped by age. Often the members of a war society carried shields bearing the same designs, and on the war trail they gave the same war cry. They also used identical body and face paints, and their war horses were decorated alike.

Nearly every Sioux tribe used bows and arrows, even after muzzle-loading guns became available. In close battle an Indian could release a number of arrows in the time it took to reload a single-shot gun. The early guns were single-shot Springfields, and it was not until after the Sioux obtained repeaters, like the Winchester '66 carbine and the Sharps .50-caliber carbine, that the bow was, to a great extent, discarded.

Among the Plains Indians the best bow makers were the Sioux and the Crow. Their bows were about four feet long, which made them handy to carry in a case attached to the quiver. They were also a convenient size for mounted warfare and for buffalo hunting. On the plains, where trees did not grow in abundance, nearly every kind of wood was used for bows. Yew and Osage orange were the best, but hard to find, and so willow, ironwood, white elm, cedar, oak, and ash were used instead.

47

The Sioux cut the wood for his bow in late winter when the sap was still down. In this condition the wood did not split while drying. Once the stave was cut and trimmed of its outer bark, the Indian rubbed it with animal fat. Then he hung it high in the lodge over the fire where the lodgepoles crossed. There the rising heat and the smoke seasoned the wood. When the stave was ready, the Indian carefully shaped it with his knife, and then rubbed it smooth with a piece of sandstone.

Most bows were straight and flat when unstrung, but some men preferred bows with a graceful curve. To obtain this curve an Indian rubbed the tapered ends well with buffalo fat, and then heated one end of the bow over the fire. When it was quite hot he placed the heated end on the ground, put his foot on it, and slowly bent it to the desired curve. Holding the bow in this position until the wood cooled made the curve permanent. The other end was bent in the same manner, but it took great patience and reheating to make the second curve exactly like the first.

To make the bow stronger, many warriors backed it with sinew. First the warrior roughened the back of the bow by scraping it with a piece of flint. Then he smeared it with a glue made by boiling scrapings of buffalo hooves or buffalo horns in a small amount of water. On top of this glue he laid a broad strip of deer or buffalo sinew, covering the full length of the bow. Thin strands of wet sinew were then wrapped around the center and the ends of the bow. The bowstring was made from twisted plant fiber or twisted rawhide.

Some warriors added a stone spearpoint to one end of their straight bow so that the bow could double as a spear.

Arrow shafts were also cut in winter. Ash, birch, and wild cherry were used, and the Indian selected branches about the thickness of a man's little finger. After he trimmed them to the proper length, he tied them into bundles of twenty or so each and, like the bow stave, hung them in the smoke of the lodge fire.

Once the shafts were well seasoned, the warrior took them down and peeled the bark carefully away. Then he scraped them smooth. To give the arrows a uniform thickness he pushed them back and forth through a hole of the proper size in the center of a flat piece of sandstone, which had been drilled for just this purpose. If a curve had developed in the shaft, the warrior rubbed it with fat, heated it, and then straightened it as it cooled.

The nock to fit the bowstring was then cut at one end. The nock was V-shaped for a fiber bowstring and U-shaped for a rawhide bowstring. At the opposite end of the arrow shaft the Indian cut a notch to hold the arrowhead. Flint, obsidian, and bone were used as points. The arrowhead was set into the deep notch and held there with glue and a tight wrapping of sinew. Hunting arrowheads were made with a base, so that it was possible to remove the arrow from the animal intact. The war arrowhead had no base. When it hit an enemy it split the shaft. Thus if a man was wounded and tried to remove the arrow, he pulled out the shaft but left the arrowhead in his body. The only way the arrow could be removed was for

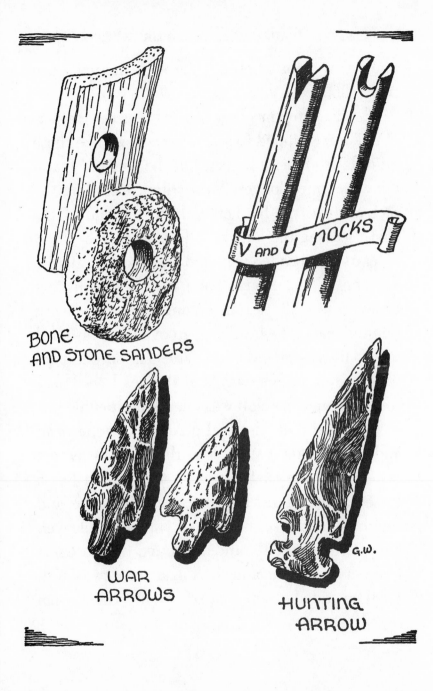

BONE
AND STONE SANDERS

V AND U NOCKS

WAR
ARROWS

HUNTING
ARROW

G.W.

another warrior to push it through the wounded man's body.

The final step in arrow making was the feathering. Three stripped feathers were used, like those on today's archery arrows, but the Indians' feathers were much longer. Most tribes, including the Sioux, glued the feathers only to the end of the shaft, leaving the long middle section free.

The stone-headed war club was another favorite weapon of the Sioux. They used three distinct types. One club had an oblong stone head with pointed ends. The head was grooved and fastened to a shaft with sinew or rawhide. The second type was made the same way, but the head was more rounded, and the club was encased in rawhide.

The third club also had a rounded stone head and a rawhide cover, but the head was not fastened to the shaft. Instead, the Indian left a loose section of rawhide between the stone and the shaft. The cover was sewed in place while wet, and when it dried the Indian wetted the loose section between stone and shaft again and twisted it. He then added a loop to fit around his wrist. When

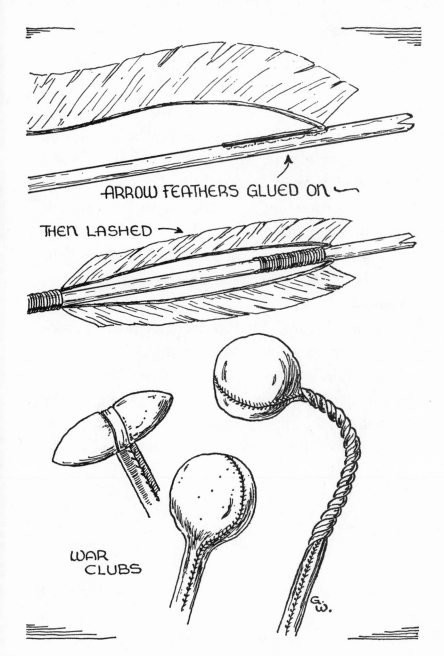

ARROW FEATHERS GLUED ON

THEN LASHED

WAR CLUBS

G. W.

this club was swung at the head of an enemy, it was a dangerous weapon.

The lance was a common Sioux weapon too. It was made like a large arrow, with the stone point set in place like an arrowhead. Contrary to some motion pictures, the Sioux did not throw the lance. It was a thrusting weapon, useful both in war and in the buffalo hunt. The lance, straight or crooked at one end, was also part of the regalia that belonged to the war societies of the Plains Indians.

A lance bent at the top like a shepherd's crook and wrapped in otter fur was the insignia of the Dog Soldiers, the Sioux tribal police. This society, made up of the bravest men of the village, ran the buffalo hunts, making sure no one started toward the herd until the proper signal was given. The members kept an eye on the sometimes hotheaded young men, to prevent them from sneaking out of camp on horse-raiding expeditions. They kept order during ceremonies and, in general, acted to enforce the tribal laws.

In battle the Dog Soldiers held the foremost

position. They carried their crooked lances with their other weapons, and they wore a long, feather-decorated sash, held over one shoulder by the strap of their bandolier. The sash was so long that when a man dismounted it trailed on the ground.

When the tide of battle turned against them, these great warriors dismounted and jabbed the sharp point of their lance through the trailing sash. Anchored to the ground by it, a Dog Soldier stood

and fought to the end. Only a man of his own tribe could free him, and one who freed himself would be forever disgraced and dishonored.

Being brave men who had gained high war honors, the Dog Soldiers were also permitted to wear a special decoration called a crow. It was worn like a bustle, hanging from the belt at the back, and was made of fur, feathers, and the whole skin of a crow. The crow was the bird that arrived on the battlefield before any other; next to come were the buzzard, the magpie, and the eagle. The feathers of these other birds, therefore, were the ones that appeared in the bustle.

Wearing their majestic war bonnet, beaded shirt and leggings, sash, and crow and carrying their crooked lance, these warriors made a striking picture.

5

THE BLACKFEET BRAVE

FROM four different directions a group of Blackfeet warriors rode into the village. All were dressed in their finest war regalia. Paint shone on the faces of those wearing war shirts and on the bodies of those who had not yet earned the right to wear the shirts. Their war horses were painted, too, and their tails were tied in knots from which eagle feathers fluttered.

As the warriors neared the center of the village

they were met by several old men and women, who were beating drums and singing a spirited war song. Led by the group of singers, the mounted men rode to the center of the village, where they gave a loud war cry and dismounted. Then the warriors danced in imitation of their prancing horses, holding their war bridles, while the horses stepped along smartly to the beating of the drums.

The following morning the fifteen braves left the village at sunup. They rode ordinary horses on the trail, leading their fast war horses so that they would be fresh and rested when they were needed.

A week later, in the distance, they sighted the enemy, a small band of Crows. The Blackfeet dismounted immediately and took shelter behind some large boulders. From parfleche cases they brought forth their splendid war regalia and costumes, together with their war medicine. Off came their everyday garments, and they donned their war costumes. A few of the men wore stand-up bonnets, which they had carried in cylindrical

rawhide cases. Broad strips of beads on their war shirts and on some leggings showed a design of three narrow diamonds, representing the three branches of the Blackfeet tribe. The men then applied war paint to themselves and to their horses.

To each warrior his personal medicine, or good-luck charm, was most important of all. Such charms usually were neck or hair ornaments. Those worn around the neck could be a buckskin bag containing herbs, a bone disc to represent the sun, a weasel skin for swiftness of movement, or possibly a bear claw for strength. Hair ornaments were worn on top of the head, at the back of the head, or tied to a braid. They were sometimes a rosette of rawhide, a large brass button, a piece of bone, or beadwork, each with a tie string for fastening it to the hair. A long buckskin thong, decorated with bone or trade beads, an ermine skin, a hair lock, or a large eagle plume, hung from the center of some hair ornaments.

Each of the Blackfeet had obtained the formula for making his medicine, together with songs to sing during battle, through the help of a dream person. A dream person was anyone who appeared in a man's dream. It could also be an animal, such as a buffalo, wolf, or coyote, which addressed the dreamer in his own tribal language. The Indian believed that during a dream his spirit left his body and followed the dream person, and he believed that whatever took place in the dream actually happened to him. Usually dream persons came to help and advise a man.

Not until the band of Blackfeet warriors were

dressed and painted did they mount their war horses and charge the enemy Crows.

If it happened that a war party was sighted by the enemy before they had time to change, they carried their clothing in its container along into battle. War regalia was believed to have protecting powers at all times, and its owner relied upon these powers even when he was not actually wearing the costume and charms. Most tribes held similar beliefs, and it was not unusual for warriors of opposing tribes to delay a battle until both sides had been given time to dress.

About two hundred and fifty years ago the Blackfeet Indians were one tribe. They lived in northern Montana and above the Canadian border. The buffalo, which migrated with the seasons and followed the spring grass north, was their main source of food. A time came when the buffalo did not move north. As the months passed and there was still no sign of the great animal, the Blackfeet chief called a council. He divided the tribe into three groups, instructing one band to go east, one

to go south, and the third band to travel westward in search of food. Only the aged remained
in the village with the head chief to await their
return.

The band that started to the east drifted far
to the north and crossed miles and miles over a
section of country burned by a prairie fire. When
finally they returned to the main camp, their
moccasins were jet black. As Indians universally
renamed things on momentous occasions, this
group was forthwith called the Siksika, meaning
"black feet."

The group that went south were the next to return. During their long absence they had acquired
a wide reputation as great fighters, having time
and time again defeated the enemy tribes to the
south. They had spread disaster among all that
had crossed their path. For their brave deeds they,
too, were renamed. The chief called them Kai-nais,
meaning "blood."

The last group to return had grown to like their
separate way of life so well that they refused to
rejoin the parent body. To these men the chief

gave the name Pia-cu-nis, meaning "cutoff," or separate. As time passed the three bands grew more individual in their habits and movements, but they kept close enough together to fight their common enemies as one unit.

Up until 1730 when the Blackfeet obtained flintlock guns, their principal weapons were war clubs, knives, and lances. The lance was the least used, and a warrior was considered a coward if his lance shaft was too long.

War clubs varied. Some were made of wood, some of elkhorn, and some had stone heads. The Blackfeet covered their stone-headed club completely, by sewing wet rawhide over it. Both mounted men and foot warriors used this weapon.

The knife, which the Blackfeet used for stabbing as well as for scalping, was a trade knife. It was introduced to the Blackfeet sometime before 1760 by Canadian traders, and was actually a butcher's knife from Sheffield, England. The Indian usually made a decorated cover in which to carry it. In the early days the knife in its scab-

64

bard was worn by the brave like a necklace, and it is said that the decorated bib at the neck opening of later war shirts was a carryover from that custom.

The Blackfeet, like the other tribes, also used the shield as a defensive weapon. Before they had horses their shields were quite large, but once the braves were mounted shields became smaller for easier handling. Not all braves, as for example the

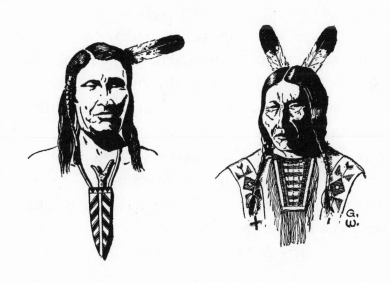

younger ones, had a shield, for it often cost a horse or two to pay the medicine man for the rituals involved. Until he could afford to buy a shield, a young man used his robe. Before going into battle he folded it over his left arm several times for protection.

The traditional enemies of the Blackfeet were the Shoshoni, the Assiniboine, the Cree, and especially the Crow. Hostilities between the Blackfeet and these tribes were kept alive by continued raids upon each other, usually for revenge or to steal horses.

The Blackfeet gave their highest tribal honor to the brave who captured an enemy's weapons, horse, or ceremonial equipment. Any warrior who had such high coups naturally stood out among his tribesmen. Parents asked him to perform the naming ceremony for their newborn baby boy. He was elected to perform special services at rituals and social affairs. These services added to the man's wealth, as he usually was given large gifts such as a horse or a buffalo robe.

In the early 1800's the Missouri Fur Company

started to construct a post at the mouth of the
Bighorn River in Crow country. The Blackfeet
thought that these white people had allied themselves with the Crow. That alone was enough to
set the Blackfeet on the war trail against them.
Then the trappers found that the Blackfeet country held finer beaver, and they moved in. After
that, no matter where they set their traps, the
hostile Blackfeet ambushed them. Time and time
again the white men were killed, and their guns,
their personal belongings, and their furs were
taken. The Indians traded the furs to the British
posts.

After a few of these raids, most of the trappers
gave up and were ready to seek their furs in less
dangerous parts of the country. For years there-
after, few white men dared enter the Blackfeet
country.

6
THE CROW INDIAN FIGHTER

THE Crow Indians were great hunters and warriors. They called themselves Absarokee, which in their language means Children of the Raven, or Raven People. The raven—not the crow—was their tribal medicine, or good-luck sign.

The Crows were divided into two groups, the Mountain Crows of southern Montana and northern Wyoming, and the River Crows who made their home along the Yellowstone River. There they were surrounded by the Blackfeet, the Sioux, the Cheyenne, the Wind River Shoshoni, and others. These tribes often infringed upon land the Crows claimed as their own hunting grounds, and, in turn, the Crows ventured into the hunting areas of their neighbors. The result, of course, was war. They were often at war with the Sioux, and always at war with the Blackfeet.

To frustrate the Blackfeet, as well as to bring the buffalo to their own range, the Crows often set fire to large sections of the dry prairie grass. They knew full well that the Blackfeet would retaliate, and so the Crow scouts, or Wolves, were constantly on the alert. When a Wolf scout was on duty he covered his head and body with a tanned wolf skin. Seen from a distance, as he squatted on his haunches atop a hill, it was hard to tell if he was an animal or a man.

Whenever a Wolf discovered an enemy approaching, he signaled the camp by flashing a small hand mirror. These circular mirrors, obtained in trade from white men, were in great demand, because they could be used in many ways. They were faster and safer for signaling than a telltale smoke signal. Fastened on a shield a mirror could, when it caught the sun, momentarily blind an enemy. A warrior also liked to admire himself in the mirror when in full war paint, and he could make an ornament out of one by pinning it to his broad fur neckpiece or some other part of his costume.

When a Wolf's signal came, the warriors at once dressed in their war clothes and readied their fast, well-trained war horses. After the horse appeared on the northwestern plains, the Crows owned more of them than any of their neighbors. Then, with their weapons ready, they mounted and gathered at the edge of the village, awaiting the war chief's command. Milling about on their spirited mounts, the Crow warriors presented a colorful and stirring picture.

The war chief was a man to whom they all looked with great respect. As a leader on horse raids he had gained a reputation for being able to see well in the dark, for keen hearing, and for his ability to move as silently as a shadow. These attributes had enabled him to return from raid after raid with many horses, and with all his men safe.

His war shirt was made from soft-tanned, cream-colored buckskin. The chest, shoulders, back, and sleeves of the shirt were decorated with broad bands of quill work. The chief's leggings were made from a scarlet Hudson Bay blanket. Around the bottom these leggings were adorned with a broad band of green cloth, decorated front and back with a beaded design. Thrown over his horse's withers was his robe. It was made of soft elk skin, tanned with the hair left on, and the flesh side was decorated with painted pictographs depicting his many war exploits. From the heels of his moccasins trailed a pair of wolf tails. They told one and all that he had counted coup on a live enemy. One other distinguishing feature of the war chief's dress gave further proof of his greatness. On his sleeves, in place of the usual fringe, he wore ermine skins. They meant that he had taken a gun away from an enemy.

The chief carried his war bonnet in a rawhide

case, to be donned later when the fighting began. Before then he wore a single eagle feather, standing straight up from the back of his head. His hair was braided in back, but in front it was arranged in a high pompadour. This pompadour, although it was worn by some Blackfeet, was typical of the Crows. In fact, in picture writing it was used to depict a Crow, and in sign language a man represented a Crow Indian by placing the back of the closed fist of his right hand against his forehead.

Vermillion was the color the chief most often used for his war paint, even though it sold for as much as four dollars per ounce at the trading post!

Over his back the great warrior slung his bow and quiver and his shield, and in his right hand he held his war flag. The flag, sometimes called a coup stick, was a rather long pole decorated with a row of eagle feathers. As a man earned his coup feathers, they were gradually added to this pole until thirty, enough for a bonnet, were assembled. New feathers, representing those on the

original flag, were used to make the bonnet, and the war flag remained intact. Even though a man had his bonnet, he still carried his war flag in battle and at ceremonies. At home, he often set the flag into the ground to the right of his tepee door.

In his belt the chief carried his stone-headed war club. It was well adapted for mounted fighting. The handle measured a good forty-two inches, which permitted him to keep some distance from his enemy.

The war chief's shield wore an undecorated covering of plain buckskin, which hid the painted designs and other ornaments. Just before going into battle, the chief removed the cover to reveal the powerful medicine to the enemy. Then he swung his shield in a great circle before him to prevent arrows from hitting him.

These shields were made from the neck hide of the male buffalo. The owner prepared the hide himself, and the decorations were applied by a medicine man. The warrior sat before the medicine man and counted his coups, while the medicine

74

man painted the designs, prayed over them, and sang war songs to give them power. For his services the medicine man was paid two good horses.

The shields carried by mounted men measured between sixteen and eighteen inches in diameter. However, when the Crow warriors got firearms, they carried much smaller shields to give themselves more freedom. The small shields were exact replicas of the large ones. As the Crow shields

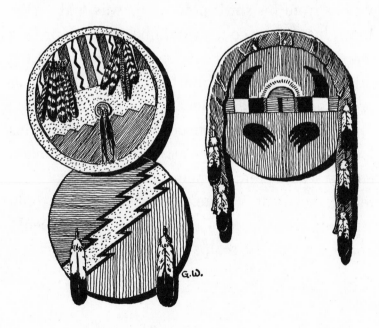

were very beautifully painted and supposed to have many powers, the Crow enemies tried to take a shield in battle even at great risk.

All the warriors in the Crow party, of course, carried their own personal war medicine with them. Their leader had a regular medicine bundle to add to his power, too.

Except for taking part in defensive warfare, as on this day, the chief never set out on the war trail unless he had a dream or vision. In those visions from his spirit powers, he was told where to go, how many coups would be counted, or how many horses his warriors would take. The vision might even reveal to him the color of the horses or the dress of their riders.

Returning from a successful raid under this leadership, the Crow warriors who had taken enemy scalps painted their faces black before entering the home village. This sign was the only announcement as a Crow brave never openly boasted about the scalps he had taken.

7
APACHE AND NAVAHO RAIDERS

Long ago the Apache and Navaho tribes of the Southwest were one people. Between the years 1200 and 1400, these Indians came down from the far north of Canada and Alaska, following a route along the eastern slopes of the Rocky Mountains. The tribes lived in small family camps instead of permanent villages, and their personal belongings were meager. A little over 400 years ago the Navaho separated from their Apache brothers.

As time passed the Apache divided further, but they still remained one tribe. The separate bands are known to us today by the names given them for some tribal characteristic or for their geographic location. They are the Mescalero Apache, the Chiricahua, the Jicarilla, the Tonto Apache, and one small band called the Lipan. (The tribes commonly known as Kiowa Apache, Yuma Apache, and Mohave Apache are not members of the Apache tribe, despite their names.)

The Apache were raiders. They raided for food, clothing, horses, guns, and slaves. To them raiding was a business, and a dangerous business, but the Apache raider was a past master at commando tactics, and he did not take needless risks. At all times he tried to raid in silence, and to obtain his objective without losing a tribesman's life. He tried not to kill those he raided. In Apache wars it was considered far better to take the enemy as slaves, and thereby enlarge the tribe. Whenever he killed in a fight, a warrior had to purify his body in the sweat lodge before he could re-enter his own encampment.

78

The Apache was not soft of heart or of muscle, however. Rigorous physical training was started in early childhood. As part of this training a man had to run several miles across the country under the blazing sun. To add to this hardship the runner was given a mouthful of water, and at the end of his run he was required to spit it out again to prove that he had not yielded to the temptation of swallowing any of it.

Young boys trained for war by standing out in the open, dodging arrows shot toward them by seasoned warriors. The boys ran down cottontails, quail, and wild turkeys for food, and they chased butterflies to learn how to dodge. Whenever a boy caught a butterfly he rubbed it on his chest, in the hope that he would gain some of its elusiveness for himself. All this training enabled an Apache to travel at a speed of four miles an hour, and to cover from thirty-five to forty miles in a day.

In enemy country the Apache concealed himself cleverly, and his patience was as great as his endurance. Hour after hour he hid behind a boulder or a clump of brush, waiting for the proper moment to spring forth to capture an enemy, his horse, or both.

Although the Apache method of attack was devious, it was not cowardly. Cochise, with less than two hundred warriors, held off the United States Army for more than ten years. He was a great leader and did not risk the life of any of his warriors in attacks on wagon trains or supply trains. He did not even attack small cavalry patrols outright; instead he literally wore them down.

A typical attack followed this pattern. From high on the rocks and cliffs an Apache band followed a group of white travelers, showing themselves from time to time, then silently vanishing again. Ahead and behind them the travelers saw smoke rising from signal fires, never knowing what it might mean. With the Apaches trailing them night and day, the nerves of the white men became frayed. They had little time for rest and even less for sleep. Water holes were few and far between, and when they finally reached one,

it was usually occupied by hostile Apache. The nights were interrupted by the howling of a coyote or the hooting of an owl. Such sounds could be genuine, but they could also be an Indian signaling to his tribesmen. No one knew for sure. When at long last nerves had been strained to the breaking point, when eyes were red-rimmed and sore from lack of sleep, and when the long night had been unusually quiet, it was time to expect a raid.

If the Apache attacked at the first sign of dawn, the white men at least had a fighting chance. If, on the other hand, the Apache silently came out of the hills during the night and stole all their horses before attacking, the travelers were at the mercy of the Indians.

When they attacked a small settlement the Apache also concentrated on breaking the settlers' nerve first. Under cover of darkness a few Apache sneaked into a small town and hid out near houses or barns. There they waited patiently for the first man to come out to do his morning chores. The Apache either took him captive or killed him. Then they faded away. Time and time again they repeated this routine—first at the edge of town, then in some other quarter, until at last the people did not dare venture from their homes after dark. When that happened, the Apache came down from their mountain stronghold to drive off the settlement's cattle, horses, and mules.

Horses and mules were especially valuable to

them, the first for riding and the second for food, as the Apache had developed a fondness for mule meat. The Apache were excellent horsemen, and small groups of them were able to raid and ter-rorize large areas. These raids, thefts, and cap-tures lasted for two hundred years. Only after the Americans arrived around 1850 was any attempt made to stop them, and this effort took forty years.

When the Apache first migrated into the South-west, one weapon they possessed was an arctic-type bow. It was of Asiatic origin, and far superior to any bow then made in their new homeland. It was sharply curved and usually made from caribou antler. The Apache also used lances, clubs, and knives in their warfare.

After the Spaniards came into the region, the Apache raided them as well as other tribes farther south for guns and ammunition. These weapons they soon learned to use to good advantage too.

The war moccasins of the Apache were peculiar to them. Made from soft buckskin or antelope skin, they had a high top reaching well above the knee. They were held up with a tie string below the knee, and the piece above was folded down over the tie. A rawhide sole extended beyond the toe, where it turned up and was cut into a small disk. This type of moccasin offered some protection against rattlesnakes, thorny plants, sand, and rocks.

Before the coming of the white men, the Apache dress was simple. A headband of buckskin held their loose hair in place, and they wore a skin shirt, breechclout, and the high moccasins. Later the Apache obtained brightly colored calico or silk on raids into Mexico and the Southwest settlements. They often made their headbands out of this material and began to wear the white man's shirt, which had a very long shirttail. One of these shirts hung almost to an Apache's knees, covering most of his breechclout. A sash, or more often a gun belt, held the shirt in around the waist. The men also began to wear vests they took during raids. They never changed their high-top moccasins, however, possibly because they found that the stiff shoes and boots of the white man were ill-suited to the terrain.

Certainly this half-Indian, half-white costume was not as colorful or romantic-looking as the costumes of most other tribes. Only the ceremonial clothes of the Apache tribe, with long fringes and some beadwork, could in any way compare with those of other Indian groups.

On the war trail each man carried a medicine charm. It, like all other sacred regalia, was made by or at least blessed by a medicine man. The medicine men also supervised all the dances performed before the warriors went on raiding expeditions or on the war trail.

The sign of the cross existed in much of the Apache symbolism, but it held no Christian meaning for them. It represented the four cardinal points and the four winds. Thus a warrior painted a cross on the foot of his moccasins before he went into strange country, in hopes that it would keep him from becoming lost.

Some of the Apache tribal regulations were rather different from those of most other tribes. One of them was for the very young, untried warrior. The first four times he was on the war trail,

he was not permitted to scratch his head with his fingers or touch his lips to water.

In such a hot, dry climate, perspiration and dust were apt to make his head itch, and he needed water. To drink and scratch without breaking the law, the warrior carried with him two implements. They hung from his belt, joined together with a thong, when not in use. One was a short scratching stick, the other a hollow drinking tube. The scratching stick was made from a piece of cedar or pine wood, and was about two and a half or three inches long. The reed was a little longer, and made from a section of cane.

The reason for these ritualistic observances has never been fully explained. They may have had a ceremonial or a religious symbolism. The Canadian Cree also used a scratching stick, but their reason was simply that they believed it was undignified for anyone to scratch his head with his fingers. The reed, at any rate, was a splendid method for drinking water from a stream, especially when no drinking vessel was at hand.

✿   ✿   ✿

As early as 1538 a Spanish priest wrote about the Navaho and called them *Apache del Navahu.*

Hunting and war were a Navaho Indian's chief objects in life. Even Navaho women went to war, and thereby gained high positions within the tribe. War usually meant a raid on one of the peaceful Pueblo tribes or on a Mexican village. The war party always brought with them a singer, who sang war chants before they set out and again when the enemy had been located. An experienced headman, whose word was law, was the leader.

Raids on other tribes were conducted primarily to capture slaves. Therefore, like their Apache brothers, the Navaho took their enemies alive whenever possible. Unlike the Apache, they did not torture their captives, though at times they did take scalps.

The earliest Navaho clothing was woven from yucca leaves and grass fibers. Later they obtained tanned skins from the neighboring Utes, and made shirts and leggings from them. These costumes did not have beadwork like those of the tribes to the north of them. Instead they were heavily decorated with beautiful silver ornaments. Working in silver was an art the Navaho learned from Mexican smiths, but they changed the Mexican designs to fit their own ceremonial needs.

The Navaho warriors often wore a buckskin head ornament that somewhat resembled the one worn by the Iroquois. At its top it held a cluster of short feathers, in the center of which were set four eagle or hawk feathers in an upright position. The rim of this cap often had a wide, thin band of hammered silver.

Another kind of cap held one or two eagle feathers, but instead of fastening them on top, the Navaho fastened them to the left side. They held them there in a horizontal position with a round or oval disk, called a concha, of silver. The lower edge of the cap was trimmed with a row of small silver buttons, and other buttons were spotted all over the crown.

The Navaho war shirt was rather short, extending just below the belt. The sleeves bore a short fringe, and the top of the shirt folded over to form

a cape rather than a collar. Around his waist the warrior wore a broad belt decorated with hand-hammered conchas and held in place with a handsome silver buckle.

The Navaho's buckskin leggings fitted him tightly, and they had fringed seams. When he was mounted the Navaho warrior wore an extra covering on his legs, made from heavier skin, for protection against cactus and thorny brush. These over-leggings folded around each leg, and they extended to the moccasins where they became broader in shape. A tie string held them just below the knee, and their entire length was buttoned with silver buttons. As a contrast to the natural tan buckskin leggings, the over-leggings were dyed a deep brick red.

The rawhide-soled moccasins of the Navaho warrior were made from thick hide, too, and left in the natural color. The soles were molded to fit around the edge of the foot and were sewed from the inside so that no stitching ever showed through the outside of the sole. The tops folded over, and they were held with small silver buttons, too. This type of moccasin is still worn today by the Navaho, even though they often wear the white man's Western shirt and blue jeans.

When the early Navaho were not engaged in raiding, and such periods were rare, sentinels guarded the hunting grounds. Stationed on high, rocky lookouts, they signaled the hidden encampment with fires by night and with smoke signals during the day.

The weapons carried by the Navaho included the spear, bow and arrows, stone ax, and rawhide shield. The shaft of the spear was from seven to eight feet long and was tipped with a point of chipped stone. It was decorated with eagle plumes, and, if the owner possessed one, with a scalp.

The bow of the Navaho was made from a single piece of oak, sumac, juniper, or greasewood. It was curved in the center, where it was wrapped with sinew from a mountain sheep or deer, and both ends of the bow were wrapped in the same way. The bowstring was a cord of twisted sinew. The Navaho warrior wore a leather bow guard to

protect his wrist from being cut by the rebound of the bowstring.

The arrow shafts were made of hardwood, and the Navaho favored wild currant or black greasewood. They tipped the shaft with arrowpoints of white flint and feathered it at the other end with eagle, hawk, crow, or turkey feathers. Down the length of the shaft they carved a double zigzag line, which represented lightning, a symbol of speed and destruction.

The Navaho made their arrow quivers from the tawny skin of a mountain lion. In battle a warrior slung his quiver over his shoulder; when he was hunting it usually hung from his belt.

Rawhide shields were round or oval. The face of the shield was painted with signs and symbols relating to war, and its edges were decorated with eagle feathers. The sun, moon, and the rainbow often appeared on a shield, and so did a bear's footprint, which was a symbol for strength. Slayer of Enemies, one of the Navaho mythological beings, was also depicted. The shield had a broad buckskin band by which it hung from the warrior's right shoulder, crossing over to his left side. The warrior held it there in his left hand with a deerskin thong fastened to the back.

The stone ax, or war club, was carried for use in close-up fighting.

Today the old war trails have grown dim with age. The signal fires have long since died, and their coals have turned to dead ashes. The warriors of long ago are now gathered together among the Sand Hills in the hereafter.

But the Indian tribes still produce warriors. Changing their buckskins and feathers for the uniform of the American fighting man, they have fought in two World Wars. Ribbons and medals have taken the place of the coup feathers of yesterday. Like their fathers before them, the Indian warriors of today fought for their country, and it is to them that this book is dedicated.